Faith

God's Blessed Assurance

PAINTINGS BY

Sandy Lynam Clough

HARVEST HOUSE PUBLISHERS
EUGENE, OREGON

I wish for you faith...
I send to you hope...
I share with you love from a joyful heart.

—SANDY LYNAM CLOUGH

Faith—God's Blessed Assurance

Copyright © 2001 by Sandy Lynam Clough
Published by Harvest House Publishers
Eugene, Oregon 97402

ISBN 0-7369-0515-4

Sandy Clough Studios
25 Trail Road
Marietta, GA 30064
1.800.447.8409

Design and production by Garborg Design Works, Minneapolis, Minnesota

Harvest House Publishers has made every effort to trace the ownership of all poems and quotes. In the event of a question arising from the use of a poem or quote, we regret any error made and will be pleased to make the necessary correction in future editions of this book.

Scripture quotations are taken from the Holy Bible, New International Version®, Copyright © 1973, 1978, 1984 by the International Bible Society. Used by permission of Zondervan Publishing House.

Printed in China.

Faith sees the invisible, believes the unbelievable, and receives the impossible.

CORRIE TEN BOOM

Faith is putting your trust in things unseen.
It can carry you through the roughest of times and
become strengthened during the best of times.
It has inspired millions to overcome insurmountable
odds. The smallest acts of faith can sometimes reap
the greatest rewards. It is the lifeline God has given
us to assure us of His infinite love, power, and mercy.

Faith can move mountains.

*Faith goes up the stairs
that love has made and
looks out of the windows
which hope has opened.*

CHARLES SPURGEON

Faith, like sight, is nothing apart from God. You might as well shut your eyes and look inside, and see whether you have sight as to look inside to discover whether you have faith.

HANNAH WHITALL SMITH

If fear is cultivated it will become stronger, if faith is cultivated it will achieve mastery.

JOHN PAUL JONES

Our faith comes in moments. . . yet there is a
depth in those brief moments which constrains us to
ascribe more reality to them than to all other experiences.

RALPH WALDO EMERSON

*The smallest seed of faith is better
than the largest fruit of happiness.*

HENRY DAVID THOREAU

8

Faith is our spiritual oxygen.
It not only keeps us alive in God,
but enables us to grow stronger.

JOYCE LANDORF HEATHERLEY

Faith is believing in things when
common sense tells you not to.

GEORGE SEATON
MIRACLE ON 34TH STREET

Cast thy bread
upon the waters:
for thou shalt find
it after many days.

THE BOOK OF ECCLESIASTES

Let us have faith that right makes might; and in that
faith let us dare to do our duty as we understand it.

ABRAHAM LINCOLN

I have fought a good fight,
I have finished my course,
I have kept the faith.

THE BOOK OF 2 TIMOTHY

Faith is like radar that sees through the fog—the reality
of things at a distance that the human eye cannot see.

CORRIE TEN BOOM

A better world shall

emerge based on faith

and understanding.

GENERAL DOUGLAS MACARTHUR

A life without faith in something is too narrow a space to live.

GEORGE E. WOODBERRY

*It is faith among men
that holds the moral elements
of society together, as it is
faith in God that binds
the world to his throne.*

WILLIAM M. EVARTS

He who loses money loses much.
He who loses a friend loses more.
But he who loses faith loses all.

HENRY H. HASKINS

We are twice armed
if we fight with faith.

PLATO

Sandy Lynam Clough 1985

We must have infinite
faith in each other.
If we have not,
we must never let it
leak out that we have not.

HENRY DAVID THOREAU

Talk unbelief, and you will have unbelief;
but talk faith, and you will have faith.
According to the seed sown will be the harvest.

ELLEN G. WHITE

*Faith is like electricity.
You can't see it,
but you can see the light.*

AUTHOR UNKNOWN

Sandy Lynam Clough

Keep your chin up
and your knees down.

ANONYMOUS

It takes vision and courage to create
—it takes faith and courage to prove.

OWEN D. YOUNG

Faith is love taking the form of aspiration.

WILLIAM ELLERY CHANNING

What lies behind us and what lies before us
are tiny matters compared to what lies within us.

RALPH WALDO EMERSON

I am not afraid of storms for I am
learning how to sail my ship.

*Be faithful in small
things because it is in them
that your strength lies.*

If you have faith as small as a mustard seed, you can say to this mountain, "Move from here to there" and it will move. Nothing will be impossible for you.

THE BOOK OF MATTHEW

Faith is different from proof; the latter is human, the former is a gift from God.

BLAISE PASCAL

When we walk to the edge
of all the light we have and
take the step into the darkness
of the unknown, we must believe
that one of two things will happen.
There will be something solid
for us to stand on or we
will be taught to fly.

PATRICK OVERTON

Faith is the substance
of things hoped for,
the evidence of things not seen.

THE BOOK OF HEBREWS

Faith is a light of such supreme brilliance
that it dazzles the mind and
darkens all its visions of other realities...

THOMAS MERTON

Faith is trusting God in
the present to do what
He promises to do in the future.

KEN MAHAYNES

The beginning of anxiety is the end of faith.
But the beginning of faith is the end of anxiety.

GEORGE MÜLLER

Faith is an action, based upon a belief that is supported by confidence.

R.W. SCHAMBACH

True Christian faith fulfills man's desires to perceive the eternal. It gives him a more extensive knowledge of all things invisible. Living faith introduces him to what the eye has not seen, nor the ear heard, nor the heart conceived in the clearest light, with the fullest certainty and evidence. Knowing these benefits, who would not wish for such faith? With faith comes not only this awareness, but also the fulfillment of the promise of holiness and happiness.

JOHN WESLEY

Faith makes all things possible, not easy.

ANONYMOUS

31

*A little faith will bring your
soul to heaven; a great faith will
bring heaven to your soul.*

D. L. MOODY